If You Won 100 Dollars

Bob McCall

Contents

The Contest 2

An Interview with a Banker 7

An Interview with a Newspaper Carrier 15

An Interview with a Working Mom 22

And the Winner Is 28

Glossary 32

Rigby

A Harcourt Achieve Imprint

www.Rigby.com
1-800-531-5015

The Contest

The new park opened in town and the mayor decided to have a contest. People would **estimate** the number of screws that were used to build the playscape. The person who got the closest without going over would receive 100 dollars and he or she would be interviewed for the newspaper. Mark, Linda, and Tim thought that 100 dollars was a lot of money, so each made an estimate. Then Mark asked his friends what they would do if they won 100 dollars.

Can you estimate how many screws it took to build this playscape?

Linda said that she would buy stamps for her collection. Then she said maybe she'd buy shoes instead. Then she said she wasn't sure *what* she'd do.

Mark and Tim didn't know what to buy. If they won 100 dollars they could get a video game or new sneakers. But they weren't sure if that was the best way to spend the money.

Tim wanted to go on a fact-finding mission to get ideas about what to do with 100 dollars. He suggested that the three of them each pick a different person to interview.

Tim wanted to interview his neighbor Mrs. Jones who works in a bank. Linda wanted to interview her older sister, Marcie, who was a newspaper carrier. Mark wanted to interview his mom because she was knowledgeable about money.

$ Spending money on new clothes and hobbies can be fun, but is it the best thing to do?

As they rode their bikes to Mrs. Jones's house, Linda reminded them to ask questions using the words that they had learned about in school: *Who, What, Where, When,* and *Why.*

$ Linda has a helmet, shoes, clothing, and a bike. She couldn't buy all of these things with a hundred dollars.

An Interview with a Banker

The three friends arrived at Mrs. Jones's house and knocked on the door.

Tim: Hi, Mrs. Jones. We were wondering if you have a few minutes to talk to us. We are entering a contest and we might win 100 dollars. We would like to know what you would do if you won 100 dollars.

Mrs. Jones: Sure, come on in. If I won 100 dollars, I would put the money in a bank.

Mrs. Jones is the bank manager who is in charge of the bank. She helps people decide what to do with their money.

7

Mark: Why would you put your money in a bank?

Mrs. Jones: The bank keeps all of the money in a bank vault. The big, thick, steel door keeps the money safe.

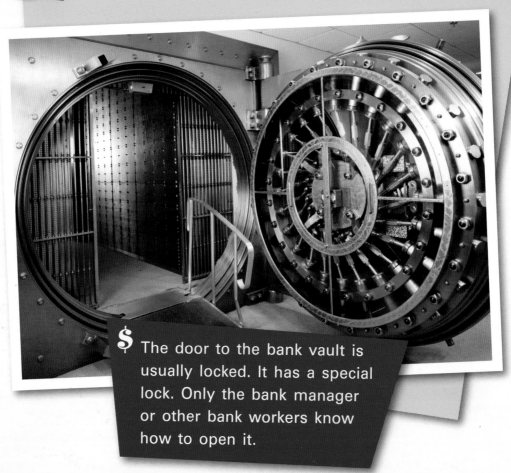

$ The door to the bank vault is usually locked. It has a special lock. Only the bank manager or other bank workers know how to open it.

Tim: How do you put money in the bank?

Mrs. Jones: First you have to open a savings account. The account has your name and a number that goes with it so the bank knows that the money in the account is yours. You also get an account book. You write the amount of money you have in your account in your account book. You can **deposit** money in your savings account any time you want.

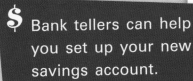
$ Bank tellers can help you set up your new savings account.

Linda: How do you deposit money?

Mrs. Jones: You give a bank teller your money and a deposit slip that says how much money you are putting in the bank. The bank teller is the person who works behind the counter. He or she will add your new deposit to the money that is already in your account.

The money you deposit is yours, even though you leave it at the bank. You can **withdraw** all of your money or part of it at any time. But the longer you leave your money in the bank, the more **interest** you will **earn**. Interest is the money the bank gives you for having a savings account. Earning interest is the best reason to save money in a bank.

BANK OF GLENVIEW
GLENVIEW BANKS LIMITED

Deposit

$ deposit slip

Paid in by _____

_____
Credit account of

Date _____
Notes _____
Coin _____
Checks _____

$ [   ]

444565532

? ? ?

$ A bank teller has to be good at math. She has to add up the amount of money deposited and the money people withdraw. She has to be sure that all the amounts are correct!

Mark: How do you earn interest?

Mrs. Jones: The bank knows how much money you have saved. They multiply how much money is in your account by an **interest rate**. To make the math easy, suppose that the interest rate is five percent. This chart shows what you would earn after one year and after two years.

Amount of Deposit	Interest at 5%	Total After 1 Year	Total After 2 years
$100.00	$5.00	$105.00	$110.25

Tim: Why will the bank pay me to keep money in a savings account?

Mrs. Jones: The bank uses your money to make more money. You're actually lending your money to the bank. Interest is what the bank gives you for letting them lend your money to others. For example, people sometimes borrow money from the bank to buy a new car or a new house.

SOLD

For Sale By Owner

4231

$ Houses cost a lot of money. Many people take out a loan from the bank to help pay for a new home.

Mrs. Jones: A person who borrows money has to pay back that amount plus interest. So part of that interest is the interest money that the bank pays you. Remember that the longer you save and the more money that you add to your account, the more money you'll earn.

The kids thought everything Mrs. Jones told them was remarkable. They thanked her for allowing them to interview her. They also decided to meet the next day to interview Linda's sister, Marcie.

$ The bank pays interest to people who save money. When you borrow money from the bank you have to pay interest.

14

An Interview with a Newspaper Carrier

The next afternoon, Linda took Tim and Mark to interview her sister.

Linda: We would like to know what you would do if you won 100 dollars.

Marcie: First I would make a chart of the things I really wanted. Then I'd see which things I could buy for 100 dollars or less.

Things I Want	Things under $100.00	Things over $100.00
a new bicycle		✔
3 CDs	✔	
pet robot dog		✔
cell phone		✔

Linda: Why wouldn't you buy something you need instead of something you want?

Marcie: Mom and Dad provide me with food, clothing, and a place to live, so I don't need to buy those things. I took a newspaper carrier job to earn money to pay for things I *want*, like a new bicycle. Bicycles can cost a lot of money.

$ Houses, clothes, and food are all basic needs.

Mark: Where do you keep your money?

Marcie: I keep the money I'm saving for the bicycle in a savings account. Every week I put my money in there. The money earns interest, which means I can get my bicycle even faster than if I kept my money at home in a drawer.

$ It's a good idea to go to the bank once a week to deposit your savings. That way it can start earning interest.

Linda: How do you stop yourself from spending the money before you have enough for the bicycle?

Marcie: It's hard to save money. My friend has a new cell phone, and she can take photos and send text messages! I have enough money for that phone right now, but I won't buy it because I really want to buy a bike.

$ It can cost 25 cents for every text message. It doesn't sound like a lot, but it can add up to over 100 dollars very quickly!

18

Mark: Do you know what kind of bike you want?

Marcie: I know exactly which kind of bike I want. I cut out a picture of it from a magazine and hung it in my bedroom. It helps me remember why I'm a newspaper carrier and why I'm saving my money.

The Trekker 2000 rides smooth and fast. Its frame is strong and can take whatever punishment you can dish out.

$ Having a clear goal can help you save money.

Linda: How much do you work?

Marcie: I get up really early seven days a week for my job because I want to get that bike. I even deliver newspapers when it's raining or snowing outside.

Mark: How long have you been saving?

Marcie: Well, I've been working for 6 months, and pretty soon I'll have enough money to buy the bike. Of course, if I won 100 dollars, I would have enough right now.

$ Delivering newspapers is hard work. The newspaper has to be delivered every day, and readers expect their papers early in the morning.

Tim: What are you going to save up for next?

Marcie: I think I'm going to save for a robot dog. It costs a lot of money, so I'll be saving for a while.

Linda: Thanks for talking to us, Marcie.

Mark's mom wouldn't be available the next day, so the three friends decided to meet in two days to talk to her.

$ A pet robot dog is a fun toy to own but it costs over 1,000 dollars!

An Interview with a Working Mom

A few days later, Linda and Tim went to Mark's house to talk to his mother.

Mark: Mom, we would like to know what *you* would do if you won 100 dollars.

Mark's mom: That's a good question. First I'd look at our **budget**.

Our Budget: May		
Monthly Household Expenses	**Amount Owed**	**Amount Paid**
House Mortgage Payment	$1000.00	$1000.00
Phone	$100.00	$100.00
Electricity	$125.00	$125.00
Gasoline for the cars	$175.00	$175.00
Food	$450.00	$450.00
Medicine	$100.00	$100.00
Clothing	$300.00	$300.00
Other	$1000.00	$1000.00
Retirement	$1750.00	$1750.00
Savings	$1000.00	$1000.00
Total	$6000.00	$6000.00

Tim: What's a budget?

Mark's mom: Our family **expenses** are part of the budget. The **income** Mark's dad and I earn pays for the things we need and want. Each month we pay for food, clothes, phone, electricity, gas, medicine, and our **mortgage**. We also pay for things like birthday parties and presents, dinners out, and trips to amusement parks. We put away money in a savings account so we'll have it if we need it. We also put money away for our retirement or when we stop working. Each month the computer program gives me a circle graph that shows what percent of our income goes where.

Our Monthly Spending

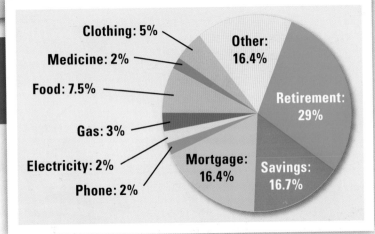

Clothing: 5%
Medicine: 2%
Food: 7.5%
Gas: 3%
Electricity: 2%
Phone: 2%
Mortgage: 16.4%
Savings: 16.7%
Retirement: 29%
Other: 16.4%

Linda: How do you know you are not spending more than you have?

Mark's mom: Every month Mark's dad and I balance the budget together. We want to make sure we don't spend more money than we have. There are always things we'd like to buy, but if we don't stick to the budget, we won't have enough money to pay our bills. However, we do have goals we set for ourselves.

$ Everyone wants to take a vacation, but it takes careful planning. When you get home, there will still be bills to pay and monthly expenses, so spending all of your money when you're away isn't wise.

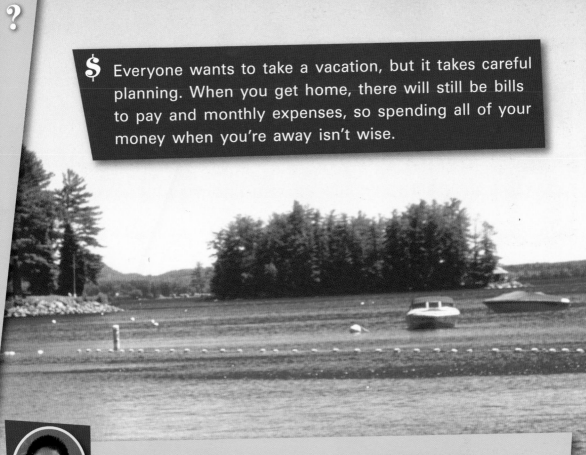

Mark: What are some of these goals?

Mark's mom: Our family trip to the beach this summer is one of those goals. Dad and I made a plan. We know how much money we need to save for the trip. If I won 100 dollars, it would probably go toward the trip.

Mark: Can you help me figure out why I don't have any money saved?

Mark's mom: Sure, we can make a circle graph to see where you spend your money.

Mark's Yearly Spending

- Movies 25%
- CDs and DVDs 50%
- New toy or game 25%

Mark: What should I do if I win the money?

Mark's mom: You always say you want that great new guitar. The guitar costs 200 dollars. I would save the 100 dollars. Then you can set up your own budget to save for the other 100 dollars. Each month when you get your allowance, you can spend some and save some. Pretty soon you'll have enough!

Linda and Tim decided that they, too, should set up their own budgets to save for things they wanted. All three children thanked Mark's mom. They were very happy that they had interviewed her and the others. They had learned a lot.

$ A brand new guitar can cost from 200 dollars to a 1,000 dollars.

And the Winner Is...

The next day, Linda, Tim, and Mark met at Tim's house to talk about what they had decided to do with the 100 dollars if they won it.

Linda decided that she would put the money in a bank to save for a computer. Mark decided to save the money for the guitar. Tim knew he really wanted a new skateboard and new gear to go with it. He'd save the 100 dollars and then begin doing small jobs for neighbors to earn the rest of the money.

The winner would be announced the next day in the newspaper. They couldn't wait to see if the newspaper would contact one of them.

By the end of the day, they realized that none of them had won. They were curious, though, to see if they knew the winner. The friends decided to meet the next morning to read the article together.

At Tim's house the next day, they opened the newspaper and began searching for the article. When they finally found it, they saw that their teacher, Mrs. Grayson, had won the 100 dollars.

Mrs. Grayson said she knew just what to do with the 100 dollars. She was going to give the money to the local library so they could buy new books.

Tim, Mark, and Linda were happy for their teacher. And they learned about something else they could do with their money. They could give it to people or places that needed it.

$ Mrs. Grayson's guess was the closest. She said the playground had 9,000 screws.

Glossary

budget a plan for how to spend your money

deposit money that is put in the bank

earn to receive money in return for doing work

estimate to make an educated guess about something

expenses money spent on a regular schedule for necessary things such as food

income money that is made through a job or other means

interest a charge, or payment, for borrowed money

interest rate the number which multiplied by your deposit gives you the amount of interest to be paid.

mortgage money paid on a house

withdraw take out